History's Greatest Mysteries: The U

By Charles Rive

The FBI's composite sketch of the suspect.

About Charles River Editors

Charles River Editors provides superior editing and original writing services across the digital publishing industry, with the expertise to create digital content for publishers across a vast range of subject matter. In addition to providing original digital content for third party publishers, we also republish civilization's greatest literary works, bringing them to new generations of readers via ebooks.

Introduction

An FBI Wanted Poster of D.B. Cooper

D.B. Cooper

"It was Thanksgiving eve

Back in 1971

He had on a pair of sunglasses

There wasn't any sun

He used the name Dan Cooper

When he paid for the flight

That was going to Seattle

On that cold and nasty night." – Chuck Brodsky, *The Ballad of D.B. Cooper*

"Maybe a hydrologist can use the latest technology to trace the $5,800 in ransom money found in 1980 to where Cooper landed upstream. Or maybe someone just remembers that odd uncle." – FBI Special Agent Larry Carr

On November 24, 1971, there was little to suggest that the skies above the Pacific Northwest would produce one of the greatest mysteries in American history and a criminal investigation that is still ongoing over 40 years later. However, on the day before Thanksgiving, a man calling himself Dan Cooper boarded Northwest Orient Flight 305 from Portland to Seattle and sat in the rear of the cabin. Shortly after takeoff, the man handed a flight attendant warning that he had a bomb and informed her that he was hijacking the plane. Cooper demanded $200,000, several parachutes, and a truck to refuel the plane when it landed in Seattle. Another flight attendant would later inform authorities, "He seemed rather nice. He was never cruel or nasty. He was thoughtful and calm all the time."

When the plane landed at Seattle-Tacoma Airport, Cooper's demands were met, after which he let all of the passengers and most of the crew off. He then told pilot William Scott to fly towards Mexico at no higher than 10,000 feet and at the slowest possible speed, which would also require a refueling stop in Reno, Nevada. About 30 minutes after the plane had taken off, Cooper manually activated the aft air staircase near the back of the cabin and apparently jumped out of the plane shortly after. The plane landed without any problems at Reno about 90 minutes after Cooper had activated the staircase to exit.

Despite leaving dozens of fingerprints, as well as a couple of personal effects, authorities could not identify Cooper, even though Cooper was being actively investigated within minutes of hijacking the plane on its way to Seattle. Furthermore, nobody was sure where Cooper landed, or if he even survived the jump, and few clues were found even after one of the most intensive manhunts in American history. Adding to the mystery is the fact that Cooper couldn't possibly have known his precise location when he jumped due to the cloud cover at 5,000 feet obscuring visibility.

Since that night in November 1971, only a little light has been shed on the mystery. In 1980, a boy playing along the banks of the Columbia River found some of the stolen money still banded together but in bad shape. This heightened the belief of many that Cooper didn't land safely, and that he may have fallen into a body of water, but the inability to locate other money and the fact that some bills were missing from the discovered packets alternatively suggest that Cooper survived the jump and intentionally buried the money.

Either way, the additional findings have only added to the intrigue and speculation over who Cooper was, and the mystery and fascination with the case has only made things more difficult, as it produced apparent copycat attempts and a host of individuals who claimed to be D.B. Cooper on their deathbeds, forcing investigators to check out and refute claims. To date, those in charge of the investigation have enough evidence to eliminate the names traditionally listed as suspects, either through fingerprints or alibis. As a result, the identity of D.B. Cooper and his fate remain unsolved, and over 40 years after he jumped out of that plane, the FBI doesn't know much too more than it did in 1971. As the FBI put it on its website in 2007, "We've run down thousands of leads and considered all sorts of scenarios. And amateur sleuths have put forward plenty of their own theories. Yet the case remains unsolved. Would we still like to get our man? Absolutely."

History's Greatest Mysteries: The Unsolved Case of D.B. Cooper comprehensively covers the facts, mysteries, and theories surrounding the only unsolved hijacking case in the United States, and speculation over the hijacker who either got away or died trying. Along with pictures and a bibliography, you will learn about D.B. Cooper and his case like you never have before, in no time at all.

History's Greatest Mysteries: The Unsolved Case of D.B. Cooper

About Charles River Editors

Introduction

Chapter 1: The Potential Background of a Man with a Plan

Chapter 2: Before Boarding

Chapter 3: In the Air to Seattle

Chapter 4: The Ground and The Jump

Chapter 5: On the Ground or In It?

Chapter 6: NORJAK

Chapter 7: The Mystery Endures

Bibliography

Chapter 1: The Potential Background of a Man with a Plan

"Who was Cooper? Did he survive the jump? And what happened to the loot, only a small part of which has ever surfaced? It's a mystery, frankly. We've run down thousands of leads and considered all sorts of scenarios. And amateur sleuths have put forward plenty of their own theories. Yet the case remains unsolved." – The FBI's website (
http://www.fbi.gov/news/stories/2006/november/dbcooper_112406)

Although he has never been positively identified, the man who boarded a Northwest Orient Airlines flight to Seattle was in all likelihood born in the Pacific Northwest in the late 1920s, information that is based on eyewitnesses' physical description of the suspect and a knowledge of the area that he mentioned while talking to flight attendants. As such, he grew up during the Great Depression, which may have meant his family suffered hardships that left him financially or emotionally deprived. For example, according to Lyle Christiansen, the brother of one of the main suspects (Kenneth Christiansen), he did not come from a very loving family. "All of us kids did not get lots of hugs when we were growing up and we missed a lot because of it. I think it made us all a little bashful and made us long for the hugs. Our folks were so busy. Pa in the field and Ma, cooking, sewing, washing clothes, canning, gardening, and also helping with the harvesting."

Based on his age and knowledge of planes, not to mention his audacious plan to parachute out of one in midair, it's likely that Cooper either served in World War II or at least wanted to. Kenneth Christiansen didn't serve in active combat, but he was in Japan after the war, and he did make training jumps. Perhaps more tellingly, Christiansen was an employee of Northwest Orient Airlines by the 1950s and he fit the age range. Christiansen was occasionally the purser (chief flight attendant) on flights, and one contemporary, Harry Honda, noted of him, "He was almost invisible. If you asked somebody on his plane who was the purser on that flight, they couldn't tell you—that's how quiet this guy was."

One suspect, Floyd McCoy, was too young to fight in World War II, but he once wrote, "During my formative years, it was still the in-thing to serve one's country so at nineteen I followed my father's footsteps and enlisted in the army. After completing parachute school and volunteering for the Green Berets, then came two more years of advanced demolition and guerrilla warfare." McCoy was singled out as a potential suspect after attempting a hijacking that was similar in style to the one Cooper pulled off just a few months earlier, and according to one army report on McCoy, the man who later became a hijacker started out as a war hero who piloted a helicopter into harm's way: "Due to the extreme danger caused by the burning aircraft plus the added danger of enemy intrusion, McCoy placed his helicopter as near as possible to the downed aircraft. With complete disregard for his own safety, McCoy leaped from the aircraft and worked his way through the dense jungle to his comrades. He immediately located the two survivors and led them to his waiting helicopter." Another report read, "Flying by instrumentation and radio alone, McCoy located the compound and came under automatic weapon and small arms fire. With the position of the compound marked by a flare and the firefight marked by tracer round, McCoy began a series of firing passes, launching rockets until his ammunition was expended. Due to his courageous flight and highly accurate fire, the enemy was completely routed, leaving twenty bodies behind."

Shortly before the Cooper hijacking, Richard McCoy was taking a class and was asked to write a paper on how best to deter hijackings. His words were chilling: "In working on the project, it was necessary to play the roles of the people involved. The person I identified most with was the skyjacker." For that and other reasons, when McCoy was killed in a shootout in 1974, the federal agent who shot him declared, "When I shot Richard McCoy, I shot D. B. Cooper at the same time." But while McCoy's own words and hijacking were evidence he may have been Cooper, authorities believe he was a copycat, and his age didn't fit the description of Cooper as someone in his 40s. Furthermore, while investigators initially assumed Cooper was an experienced parachutist, maybe even an expert paratrooper, this belief has since been revised based on the conditions that night. FBI Special Agent Larry Carr pointed out, "We originally thought Cooper was an experienced jumper, perhaps even a paratrooper. We concluded after a few years this was simply not true. No experienced parachutist would have jumped in the pitch-black night, in the rain, with a 200-mile-an-hour wind in his face, wearing loafers and a trench coat. It was simply too risky. He also missed that his reserve chute was only for training and had been sewn shut— something a skilled skydiver would have checked." Ironically, Christiansen's training in skydiving has also led the FBI to conclude he wasn't actually Cooper.

Special Agent Larry Carr

Although Cooper was clearly of fighting age at the time of World War II, one of the most interesting aspects of the case is that his fingerprints didn't match any in the files, which included the fingerprints of military personnel. Of course, that only deepens the mystery, because if Cooper was not a criminal or in the military, then who was he and how did he come up with his audacious plan?

While it's impossible to know Cooper's motives, the elements of the hijacking make clear what he was thinking in terms of a plan. In terms of picking a target, the new style of Boeing 727, the 100, was just the right size and had a feature that would enable him to make a clean getaway. Since the suspect would easily be apprehended on the ground, the only thing to do was to leave the plane while it was still in the air, an escape route made possible by the releasable staircase in the rear of the 727. Cooper knew how to open the plane's side door, so if he could also deploy the stairs, he could jump from the bottom step and safely clear the plane's engines. As FBI chief investigator Ralph Himmelsbach later explained, "The 727 became notorious through this case because it is the only airliner from which a successful parachute jump can be made from the passenger cabin."

A Boeing 727 with the aft staircase down.

Threatening a plane with a bomb was nothing new for hijackers at the time, so that was a good way to quickly get and keep the attention of a flight crew. It's unclear whether Cooper knew how to make a bomb or whether the device he ended up showing a flight attendant was anything more than a series of harmless wires, but it would get the job done.

Jumping out of a plane around 10,000 feet would obviously require parachutes, and Cooper had to be wary of being intentionally supplied with parachutes that would fail. Whether he was experienced or not, it seems he knew that skydivers wore two chutes: a primary one on their backs and a secondary one on their chests.

With those main elements in place, the suspect likely came up with an alias and had to determine how much ransom money to ask for. It was reported that Cooper ended up asking for $200,000 in $20 bills, leading at least one writer to believe Cooper had thought it out. Richard Krajicek of CrimeLibrary.com notes, "Cooper had specified $20 bills—an indication of his attention to detail in the planning. He apparently had calculated that 10,000 $20 bills would weigh just 21 pounds. Smaller denominations would add weight and danger to his skydive. Larger denominations would be more conspicuous and therefore more difficult to pass. Cooper specified the bills should have random, not sequential, serial numbers." But like so much else in the case, other sources have claimed Cooper never specified the denomination of the bills, only that they be "negotiable American currency".

One of the few hard facts in the case is that the suspect gave his name as Dan Cooper, but it's unclear why or how he came up with that name. Coincidentally or not, there was a well-known contemporary comic artist named Dan Cooper who drew a series of comics about a Canadian military ace pilot, as well as the pilot of spaceships. Some of Cooper's comics depicted a character jumping out of a plane in a parachute, and the delivery of ransom money in a knapsack, which matched some of the details of the hijacking. Since the comic artist was French-Belgian and writing about a Canadian character, people looking for any tentative clue speculate that the hijacker may have been familiarized with Cooper's work while in Europe during World War II or may have been Canadian.

Taking all of the known facts together, Carr, the special agent currently in charge of the investigation, has a relatively simple profile of the suspect, which can still be found on the FBI's website:

> "He served in the Air Force and at some point was stationed in Europe, where he may have become interested in the Dan Cooper comic books.
>
> He worked as a cargo loader on planes, giving him knowledge and experience in the aviation industry, which was in its infancy in 1971.
>
> Because his job required him to throw cargo out of planes, Cooper would have worn an emergency parachute in case he fell out. This would have provided him with working knowledge of parachutes but not necessarily the functional knowledge to survive the jump he made.
>
> He may have come from the East Coast, but taken an aviation job in Seattle when he got out of the military. It's possible he lost his job during an economic downturn in the aviation industry in 1970-71. If he was a loner with little or no family,

'nobody would have missed him' after he was gone."

Chapter 2: Before Boarding

"American authorities were loath to make sweeping changes in air security, even after the trio of hijackings to Jordan. President Nixon ordered the usual response of armed sky marshals on some flights. More aggressive measures, including baggage inspection and metal detectors, were rejected as being bad for the air travel business: They would make passengers jittery.

Against that backdrop, Dan Cooper was able to walk unchallenged aboard Flight 305 with a bomb—or what he claimed was a bomb—even though everyone in the air travel industry understood that the lack of security meant any individual passenger could take down a plane." – Richard Krajicek, CrimeLibrary.com

On November 24, 1971, Cooper prepared to put his plan into motion. It seems he had even chosen the date carefully, because airlines would be incredibly busy and distracted by the many people flying home for the holidays. As he got dressed that morning, he donned a black suit and a carefully pressed white shirt, along with a somber black necktie that was clipped with his mother-of-pearl tie pin to hold it in place. He dropped a bottle of Benzedrine pills in his pocket, just in case the crew later had problems staying awake, and then he put on polished loafers and a black raincoat. He also tucked a pair of dark sunglasses in his pocket. In essence, Cooper was portraying an image that suggested there was nothing special about him, but it was the conservative business image that drew the attention of at least one airline employee, because by 1971, men's fashions had changed and color and pattern were the order of the day. Hal Williams would later tell the FBI, "Yes, as a matter of fact, there was a gentleman that looked awfully suspicious." That said, as FBI agent Himmelsbach noted, "He was your typical businessman, a suit, tie, a raincoat, carrying an attaché case. Nothing distinctive about him except perhaps for the fact that everything was very dark, black tie, black raincoat, black shoes. He appeared at the ticket counter, bought his ticket and just gave the name Cooper."

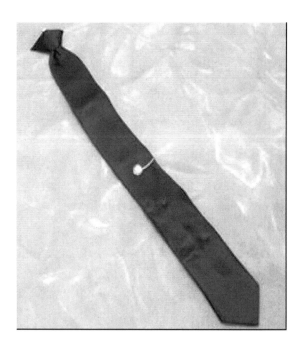

The tie that Cooper wore during the hijacking.

Cooper likely took a cab to the airport, since no car connected with him was ever found. Dennis Lysne, who was working the ticket desk at Portland International Airport that afternoon, had already worked a long day. It was mid-afternoon on the day before Thanksgiving, one of the biggest flying days of the year, and from the time he had come on duty, he had been inundated with all sorts of concerns. Lysne had to deal with elderly women asking him if it really was safe to fly, young mothers concerned about how their babies would handle the pressure changes in the cabin, and businessmen anxiously worrying about making a connecting flight.

Cooper approached Lysne not long before the flight was ready to take off and asked, "Can I get on your flight to Seattle?" Cooper then asked Lysne, "That's a 727, isn't it?" After that was verified, Cooper paid for his $20 ticket with cash. Lysne later wondered if he had missed something that he might have caught had it been a quieter day, but the man who called himself "Dan Cooper" seemed like just another hurrying businessman wanting to catch a flight for the holiday. He was not tall, at least not for a man, nor was he particularly heavy or menacing in any way. He wore comfortable looking loafers and a black raincoat, a common practice for anyone living or working in Seattle. His mother-of-pearl tie pin was well shined, and his black attaché case appeared to be clean and might even have been new. It also did not strike Lysne as odd that Cooper only needed a one way ticket, especially a flight from Portland to Seattle that was almost too short to be of any consequence.

Having purchased his ticket, Cooper made his way to the waiting area, and while other passengers waiting to board Flight 305 chatted in a little group, he stood by himself. When his turn came to board the Boeing 727-100, which was only carrying about three dozen passengers and was thus mostly empty, Cooper took seat 18C near the back of the aircraft and settled in. He laid his attaché case on the seat next to him and lit a cigarette, still a common practice on airplanes during the early '70s. He then asked the stewardess, Florence Schaffner, to bring him a bourbon and 7 Up. When she told him it would be a dollar, he handed her $20 and told her it was the smallest bill he had. She took the large bill and promised to get him his change after she served the other passengers.

Chapter 3: In the Air to Seattle

"The two flight attendants who spent the most time with him on the plane were interviewed separately the same night in separate cities and gave nearly identical descriptions. They both said he was about 5'10" to 6', 170 to 180 pounds, in his mid-40s, with brown eyes. People on the ground who came into contact with him also gave very similar descriptions." – Special Agent Larry Carr

"He wasn't nervous. He seemed rather nice. He was never cruel or nasty. He was thoughtful and calm all the time." - Flight Attendant Tina Mucklow

The plane took off on schedule around 2:50 p.m., and just minutes after the plane was in the air, Schaffner was walking past Cooper when he handed her a note. Figuring it was nothing out of the ordinary, she all but ignored the note as she dropped it in her purse; Cooper hadn't taken into account that Schaffner got love notes from her passengers all the time, to the extent that she had actually taken to wearing a wig when she worked. As a result, she merely assumed Cooper had given her his number and wasn't going to take the time to read it right then.

Florence Schaffner

Since the note was the first step in his plan, Cooper had to get her attention, so he said to her, "Miss, you'd better have a look at that note. I have a bomb." Schaffner slit open the envelope and pulled out the sheet of heavy stationary. Written neatly in all capital letters with a felt tip pen, the letter read, "I have a bomb in my briefcase. I will use it if necessary. I want you to sit next to me. You are being hijacked." She looked down at Cooper, who was looking up at her expectantly with no sense of fear or urgency, and immediately thought it was a joke. Anyone passingly familiar with the industry knew hijackers were usually political refugees or bomb throwers, not nicely-dressed businessmen drinking bourbon and 7 Up.

"You're kidding, right?" she asked.

"No, miss. This is for real."

Schaffner sat down in the empty seat next to him, just as he asked. Still hoping it might be some sort of sick joke, she asked to see the bomb, so Cooper opened the attaché case just enough to show her his creation. What Schaffner saw was a device that seemed to include a large battery and cylinders attached to wires. Seeing the look of horror on her face, he stroked the copper wire as if he might detonate it right there. She later recalled, "I saw a big battery with six dynamite sticks wrapped around the battery. And he said to me, 'All I have to do is attach this wire to this gadget here and we'll all be dead.'" Himmelsbach later theorized that Cooper got the design for the bomb from watching the famous movie *Airport*, which came out just half a year earlier.

The flight was only 30 minutes long, so Cooper had to keep things moving. As he slipped on his sunglasses, he quietly told Schaffner, "Take this down." After getting a pen from her purse, she took down the following message: "I want two hundred grand by five p.m., in cash. Put it in a knapsack. I want two back parachutes and two front parachutes. When we land, I want a fuel truck ready to refuel. No funny stuff, or I'll do the job. No fuss. After this we'll take a little trip." However, when Schaffner told him she had to take the note to the cockpit, he became suspicious, presumably because he wanted her to keep sitting near him or at least remain where he could keep an eye on her. On the other hand, he had to get the note to the captain somehow. Another stewardess, Tina Mucklow, offered to take it, but he didn't trust her either.

When Schaffner again insisted that she had to go to the cockpit, he agreed this time, saying, "All right. Go ahead." Schaffner later remembered what she was thinking as she informed the crew in the cockpit, "We were very, very scared to death. All of us were. I was thinking about dying. That's all I thought. I was also thinking, 'I'll never see my parents, my brothers and sisters." A few minutes later, Captain William Scott radioed Northwest Flight Operations across the country in Minnesota: "Passenger has advised this is a hijacking. En route to Seattle. The stew has been handed a note. He requests $200,000 in a knapsack by 5:00 PM. He wants two back parachutes, two front parachutes. He wants the money in negotiable American currency. Denomination of the bills is not important. Has bomb in briefcase will use it if anything is done to block his request."

Tina Mucklow

Captain William Scott

Once authorities on the ground were alerted, it was up to the airline to decide whether they wanted to pay the ransom. Himmelsbach explained, "The FBI asked the airline what their approach to the hijacking was going to be, that is, did they wish to pay the ransom. This is an option that the victim of extortion has rather than law enforcement, and they responded instantly that they wished to pay the ransom. And so the FBI at Seattle set about assisting in obtaining the money."

While Schaffner was gone, Mucklow took her place sitting with Cooper, and by the time Schaffner returned, he ordered another bourbon and 7 Up. When she brought it to him, he reflexively pulled out his wallet and paid for the drink, which understandably baffled the stewardess given that he was in the middle of hijacking the plane for $200,000. Noticing the look of surprise on her face, he smiled a wry smile and told her to keep the change. She then asked him where he'd like to go, but he did not answer, likely wanting to keep his plan under wraps for as long as possible.

Though he knew what he wanted and was obviously determined to get it, Cooper had nothing against Schaffner or anyone else on board. In fact, he hoped to make the entire experience as easy as possible for everyone concerned, and he even took into account the possibility that his plan would require the flight crew to work through their normal meal time. With that in mind, he told Schaffner to be sure to order extra flight meals for crew members when they landed in Seattle. There was no need for them to go hungry.

The next issue that came to Cooper's attention was whether the passengers should be alerted about the hijack. Cooper must have already considered this, as he told the pilot not to alert them but instead come up with some plausible story about the reason for the delay. Thus, Scott got on the intercom and calmly said, "Ladies and gentlemen, there's been a slight mechanical problem. We've been asked to circle Seattle to burn off excess fuel."

As he sat in his seat enjoying his second drink, one can only imagine what was running through Cooper's head as things were falling into place, at least thus far. The captain had done what he was told, as had the stewardesses, and the announcement meant he didn't need to worry about the passengers. While he couldn't yet have known what kind of activity was going on among authorities and airline officials on the ground, he likely assumed that the pilot was in constant contact with them. It seems Cooper was worried that radio signals could accidentally detonate the bomb, or at least he wanted to convey that possibility, because he ordered Mucklow to contact the captain and express his concern about the radio currents. Scott did not know if the radio might set the bomb off or not, but he knew he had to keep in touch with the ground, and furthermore, his communications hadn't triggered anything yet anyway.

By this time, the FBI was on the line, and the following dialogue took place:

Agent: "Do you know where he wants to go?"

Scott: "Negative. Have asked him once and so we don't want to ask him again. Would suggest we wait and see where he wants to go."

Agent: "Can bring out the manuals to Alaska if you think so."

A few minutes later, someone asked if Cooper could hear the radio transmissions. Scott replied, "I don't know. I think it's free to call us. Nobody's giving us any trouble up here. He's in the back."

Not only was Cooper in the back, he was enjoying his flight more than most of his fellow passengers, who were understandably nervous about the delay in landing. While they worried about making their next flights or getting on the ground safely, he was flirting with Mucklow. When he pulled out another cigarette, he offered her one as well, and after she took it, the two began a friendly conversation. When Cooper asked where she was from, Mucklow replied that she grew up in a Philadelphia suburb but was now living in Minneapolis. To that, Cooper replied, "Minneapolis is very nice country."

Mucklow next tried to make a joke that would also possibly elicit information at the same time. She told Cooper, "You know Northwest Orient has strict policies against traveling to Cuba. Can't bring home rum or cigars. Customs confiscates them in the airport." Cooper laughed and told her, "No, we're not going to Cuba. But you'll like where we're going." At that point, their conversation was interrupted by a large man in a cowboy hat who demanded to know what was going on and when they would land. For reasons that he did not understand, the cowboy's confusion amused Cooper, but once the hijacker grew tired of the interruption, he told the guy to go back to his seat. Then he turned to Mucklow and menacingly warned, "If that's a sky marshal, I don't want any more of that." She quickly reassured him, "There aren't any sky marshals on the 305 flight." Satisfied, he moved on to his next subject, telling Mucklow to call Schaffner and tell her to bring his note back, perhaps because he didn't want authorities to have any samples of his handwriting.

While the two were talking, Schaffner stopped by to tell Cooper that the company was working to get together the items he asked for, including the parachutes, which they were getting from a local military base. Cooper balked at that because he knew that military chutes had automatic opening mechanisms that gave jumpers no control over how long they fell before deploying the canopy. He told Schaffner to return to the cockpit and tell the captain in no uncertain terms that he wanted civilian parachutes with manual controls. In the end, authorities had to get the parachutes from a civilian skydiving school The fact that he had asked for two sets of parachutes had also alarmed those on the ground, because it seemed to indicate that he would keep a hostage and possibly make them jump. That possibility would ensure that the authorities would provide parachutes that actually worked, which is something Cooper may very well have had in mind when he made the demand.

Meanwhile, Cooper returned to his conversation with Mucklow, which included a comment that the airline company had probably gotten the parachutes from McChord Air Force Base since it was only 20 minutes from the Seattle-Tacoma Airport. That knowledge would later lead investigators to assume he was a local or that he was at least intimately familiar with the area. Remembering her training, Mucklow kept him talking, but when she asked him where he was from, he refused to tell her. Then she tried a different path, asking him, "Do you have a grudge against Northwest?" This question seemed to catch him off guard, and he answered quietly, "I don't have a grudge against your airline, Miss. I just have a grudge."

Suddenly, Cooper's hand jerked up, possibly due to the pent up tension he had been trying so hard to hide. He sloshed some of his drink out of his glass and Mucklow jumped a little, startled by the action. He then asked her what time it was. He knew it must be nearly 5:00, but he had not worn a watch. Looking out the window, he noted that they were "over Tacoma now", evidence that he had flown over this part of the country in the past and was familiar with the landscape. When Mucklow told Cooper it was a little after 5:00, he became panicked and asked her if the federal agents were trying to trick him, adding, "they're not gonna take me alive." Worried, Mucklow called the cockpit to see what the holdup was. Scott replied that two of the parachutes were not at the airport yet and added, "Ask him if he wants to start our descent without the chutes present." When asked, Cooper replied, "Yes." Around 5:24 p.m., authorities on the ground let Scott know that they had all of the parachutes and the money (which had been photographed and stored on microfilm for efforts to subsequently trace it), and moments later, the captain called to the back of the plane, "The front chutes are now at the airport. We're going down."

Chapter 4: The Ground and The Jump

"Out a little service doorway
In the rear of the plane
Cooper jumped into the darkness
Into the freezing rain
They say that with the windchill
It was 69 below
Not much chance that he'd survive
But if he did where did he go?" – *The Ballad of D.B. Cooper*

Cooper must have conducted research about prior hijackings and studied how other hijackers were brought down by police, because he had very specific instructions about what would happen on the ground. First, he ordered Scott to land the plane on a little used tarmac far from the main building, and he then insisted that the pilot turn off all the lights in the plane, which would preclude the possibility of having snipers target him. It was a wise choice, because the FBI later admitted "there were FBI agents with scoped rifles who were prepared, if the indications were present, that required it to pick him off."

Cooper had already warned Northwest that they were not to try to approach the plane with any type of vehicle, so the employee who had been chosen to deliver the parachutes and the money had to lug the heavy loads on foot. Adding insult to injury, that man was none other than Al Lee, Northwest Orient's Seattle operations manager. A Federal Aviation Agency official was also on hand and asked to come aboard to let Cooper know the consequences of hijacking an airplane, but he refused the request.

By this time, Cooper had grown most comfortable with Mucklow. A devout Christian, she had been able to use her faith to steady her nerves and interact with him on a personal level, and while he naturally didn't trust anyone very much, their conversations had led him to at least trust her a little more than the other members of the crew. He instructed her to open the main door of the plane, deploy the staircase and meet the airline employee halfway down the stairs. Under Cooper's penetrating gaze, she made the longest short trip of her life down and then back up the staircase, bringing the bag of money.

When he saw it, Cooper grew angry; he had specifically asked that the money be placed in a knapsack and this was an open cloth bag. However, he quickly regained his composure and checked out the bills. Looking at Mucklow, he commented gruffly, "Looks okay." In a fit of nervous tension, Mucklow joked, "There's a lot of cash in that bag. Can I have some?" Taken aback, Cooper actually reached back into the bag and tried to give her a bundle of the money. Surprised and embarrassed, she quipped, "Sorry, sir. No tips. Northwest Orient policy."

Next, Cooper instructed her to go back down the stairs and bring up the parachutes. When she complained that they would be too heavy for her, he cut her off, saying, "They aren't that heavy. You shouldn't have any trouble." It took her two trips, but she finally got the parachutes on board. She then pleaded for the passenger's safety, imploring, "Why not let them go now? You still got the crew and the plane."

Once everything he asked for was on board, Cooper gave permission for the other 36 passengers to leave the plane. He watched calmly as they all left, "decently and in order," before allowing Schaffner and another flight attendant to leave also. When told they could go, the women surprised him by timidly asking for their purses. Cooper laughed and replied, "Sure, I'm not going to bite you." He then looked at Schaffner and invited her to take hold of the money bag for a moment. Much to his delight, she lifted it slightly out of his hands before declaring, "It is heavy."

As the other women left, Cooper again became angry, this time because he noticed that the fuel was not being pumped into the plane. He turned to Mucklow and ordered, "Close the shades." He then began to complain again about the bag the federal agents had put the money in. Before Mucklow knew what was happening, Cooper began cutting one of the four parachutes apart and cannibalizing its rope and fabric to bundle the money in. While authorities on the ground couldn't have realized it, Cooper's actions had just made clear that the second set of parachutes would not be used to make a hostage jump.

Having tied up his ill-gotten money, Cooper became calm again and began giving his next batch of instructions to Mucklow: "We're going to Mexico City or anyplace in Mexico. Gear down, flaps down. You can trim the flaps to fifteen. You can stop anywhere in Mexico to refuel, but not here in the United States. Cabin lights out—no one behind the first-class curtain…The aft door must be open and the stairs must be down."

These instructions, especially the specific mention of keeping the wing flaps at 15 degrees, suggested Cooper was impressively familiar with aerodynamics and flying, and he even told the pilot he had an altimeter on his wrist that could measure altitude. Still, these final instructions posed a problem; after consulting with airline engineers, the pilot informed Cooper that they could not safely take off with the back staircase down. Cooper relented and told them they could keep the staircase up while taking off, so long as the pilot didn't pressurize the cabin once they were in the air. Having gotten this far, Cooper obviously did not want to be sucked out of the plane the moment he lowered the aft stairs.

While this was going on, the fueling was still taking place and Cooper was growing increasingly impatient. At one point, he complained, "It shouldn't take this long." As soon as he saw the fuel truck pull away, he was on the phone to the cockpit yelling, "Let's get the show on the road." Hoping to mollify him, Mucklow tried to give him the instructions on how to secure his parachutes, but he waved her away, growling, "I don't need that." She then asked him to let her go to the front of the plane, away from where he was about to open the door. He refused but assured her that as soon she showed him how to lower the stairs, she could join the rest of the crew in the cockpit. When Mucklow suggested to him that she didn't think the stairs could be lowered while the plane was in the air, he immediately snapped back at her that she was wrong, which again made clear that he knew quite a bit about the Boeing 727. Mucklow subsequently showed him how to lower the stairs and even reminded him that the plane carried oxygen if he thought he would need it. He replied, "Yes, I know where it is. If I need it I will get it." He then told her to extinguish all the lights inside the plane.

When Cooper again complained that the plane was not moving, Mucklow informed him that the pilots were filing their flight plan, to which he replied impatiently, "Never mind. They can do that over the radio once we get up." Sensing that her time with him was near an end, Mucklow asked him one more question, and undoubtedly the question she was most interested in having him answer: what was he going to do with the bomb? After a day of decisive responses from her captor, she shuddered to hear his nonchalant answer: "Take it with me, or disarm it." However, she had little time to stand there fretting, as he quickly turned to her and said, "Go to the cockpit. Close the first-class curtains. Make sure nobody comes out." She was only too happy to comply.

Now alone for the first time since he boarded the plane, Cooper removed his necktie and unbuttoned the top button of his shirt. He then used more of the parachute line to tie the money securely to his chest and crouched near the door as he waited for the plane to take off. A few minutes later, around 7:45 p.m., the plane lurched back into the air, about 2 hours after it had landed in Seattle.

Cooper waited until the plane's ascent stabilized before turning the switch to lower the aft stairs, only to have it not work. Frustrated, he called the cockpit to ask for help, but before he heard a reply, he tried one more time. This time the switch worked and the stairs lowered, allowing the wind to whip through the cabin. At this point, the plane jolted noticeably jolted down and people's ears popped in the cockpit. Hearing the roaring sound coming from the main cabin, Scott called and asked, "Can you hear me? Is there anything we can do for you?" Cooper replied tersely, "No." Another officer called a few minutes later and asked, "Everything okay back there?" Again, Cooper replied, "Everything is okay."

For all of the meticulous planning that had gone into the hijacking, it seems Cooper had failed to consider how cold it would be to jump out of a plane at that altitude, because he was about to freefall in -7 degree air and icy rain wearing nothing but a business suit, loafers, shoes, and a raincoat. Nevertheless, the moment had come, and regardless of whether Cooper was cold or not, he clearly felt it was too late to back out. With the plane flying slightly under 200 miles per hour, Cooper jumped out with two of the chutes, the money, and his clothes (aside from his tie). He also took the "bomb" with him or threw it out of the plane. When he left the steps and jumped, he entered the black abyss of a stormy northwest Pacific night in which lightning provided the only break in the darkness. As Geoffrey Gray noted in *New York* magazine, "The cloud ceiling that night was 5,000 feet, and some of the most rugged terrain in this country was beneath it: forests of pine and hemlock and spruce, canyons with cougars and bears and lakes and white-water rapids, all spilling out into the Pacific."

The plane landed without incident in Reno around 10:15, an estimated 2 hours after Cooper jumped. Law enforcement had tried to keep track of Cooper's movements by using a couple of planes to monitor the hijacked plane from above and below, but the plane's slow rate of speed made it hard for the Air Force's fighter jets. By the time a slower plane used by the National Guard joined the chase, it's believed that Cooper had already jumped.

Chapter 5: On the Ground or In It?

"Diving into the wilderness without a plan, without the right equipment, in such terrible conditions, he probably never even got his 'chute open." - FBI Special Agent Larry Carr.

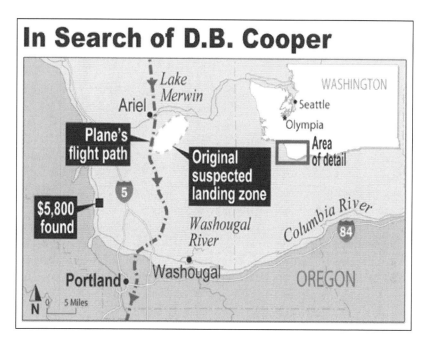

In Search of D.B. Cooper

Lake Merwin
Ariel
Plane's flight path
WASHINGTON
Seattle
Olympia
Original suspected landing zone
Area of detail
$5,800 found
5
Columbia River
84
Washougal River
Portland
Washougal
OREGON
N   0   5 Miles

At the point he jumped, the story of D. B. Cooper either ended almost immediately or continued into its next stage. If it ended, a scenario embraced by many FBI agents, including Richard Tosaw, this is likely the way in which it happened: "Disoriented by the speed with which he was falling, Cooper was unable to find the rip cord and his chute failed to open. Or he found the rip cord, but pulled it at the wrong moment and it tangled around him. Or his chute opened but he was unable to control the speed and direction of his descent, since he had rejected the more superior military parachutes in favor of the less manageable manual chutes. But in the end, little to nothing slowed his fall. Instead of floating gently to the ground as he envisioned, he tumbled head over heels until he passed out from oxygen deprivation and shock."

If Cooper didn't survive the jump, that is the kindest version of such a scenario because it means that he was either unconscious or dead by the time his body slammed into the ground or possibly a body of water like the Columbia River. Many researchers believe that most of the money which he had tied to his body remained with his body as it sank into the dark waters and was carried downstream. As it was swept along, it was beaten over and over against rocks and limbs, but some of the money finally came loose and washed up on shore, where it would be found in 1980. However, most of the $200,000 remained tangled in the parachute as the body was dragged along the riverbed until it finally lodged in a particularly deep spot. Over the next months, the remains of D. B. Cooper may have become fish food, and whatever remained could have been consumed by bacteria, leaving nothing but bones to be buried in silt at the bottom of the river. As Tosaw would later assert, "I'm convinced he's on the bottom of the Columbia River. I have no doubt that his skeleton will be found there, along with his parachutes and the rest of the money."

FBI agent Himmelsbach believed that even if Cooper initially survived the jump, he was likely hurt by the time he landed and wouldn't have lasted long: "My feeling is he would've have been hurt regardless of what he landed into. I think that Cooper mostly crawled to a creek. He didn't have any water supplies, didn't bring any along with him, and he would've had to have water to survive. So I assume he made his way to a little creek and perished there."

Captain Scott also believed that no one could have survived a jump from that height on such a terrible night. While he refused to talk to the press, after his death his widow admitted to one reporter, "He felt he jumped into Lake Merwin and got tangled up in dead trees and died." There is some pretty significant evidence to support Scott's belief, most notably the story told by Elsie Rodgers of Cozad, Nebraska. She used to entertain her grandchildren with tales of how she one found a human skull on the banks of the Columbia River in Washington State. They were both dazzled and disbelieving until, a few days after her death, they found a human skull stored neatly away in a hat box in her attic. Her children immediately turned the skull over to the FBI, but the Bureau was unable to draw any sort of definitive conclusion about its origins.

Perhaps surprisingly, many Americans hoped Cooper lived. Americans in the early '70s embraced the anti-hero, and in the minds of many people, D. B. Cooper was not a thief but a hero. After all, he had not harmed anyone and had successfully struck a blow on behalf of commoners against big business. fact, if he did survive, he likely would have found plenty of people to help him evade the police, for as one otherwise law abiding citizen put it, "You know, it's funny. Folks are actually pulling for this man. That's all anybody wants to talk about. I hear it all day long. 'Hope he made it, he deserves it, hope he gets away with every nickel.' Like he's some kind of Robin Hood character. He was John Doe. He wasn't some wild radical ... He was you or me or your neighbor." Historian Walt Crowley agreed, telling the *Seattle Times*, "It's that desperado mystique. It was an extraordinary audacious act to lower that rear gangway in flight and jump into a dark and stormy night. He didn't hurt anybody ... and we all love a mystery."

Naturally, the FBI's lead investigator, Ralph Himmelsbach, disagreed, labeling Cooper "a rodent," "a bastard," "a dirty, rotten crook", and "nothing more than a sleazy, rotten criminal who jeopardized the lives of more than 40 people for money." In case anyone did not understand what he meant by these remarks, he later added, "That's not heroic. It's selfish, dangerous and antisocial. I have no admiration for him at all. He's not at all admirable. He's just stupid and greedy." In a less inflammatory manner, Himmelsbach noted, "When a guy like that drops out of sight the people around him are glad and they don't think much about it, maybe figuring he's in jail again. You certainly don't get a 48-year-old man who has lived a normal life suddenly doing what this guy did."

Himmelsbach believed that Cooper died during his jump or soon after, but that never stopped him from looking, chasing down every tip that would come in. He would admit, "Every so often one (of these) would come along, and I'd get the rush of adrenaline. There's a guy in a bar with a bunch of $20 bills, he's limping on one leg and someone asks where he got the roll, and he says he might have hijacked an airplane. You track those things down, and they just burn out."

At least one parachute expert believes Cooper very well may have survived and pegged his odds at 50%. Frank Heyl offered some alternatives: "Let's say he went down in the water. You've gotta know how to manage that parachute. You can use it for some floatation. Now his life expectancy is not going to be very long in that water. It's cold and you have to think of the time of the year it was in, so he had probably a very, very few minutes to get on shore. But I think he could've done this." As for those who are certain Cooper was unprepared and inexperienced, Heyl added, "We don't know what he wore under the suit, could've had a pair of long underwear on which he certainly should have had. And what he had in pockets may have been the most important thing because this would've given him the tools of survival. As long as a man's got a knife, a cigarette lighter and the clothes on his back, he could've lived indefinitely out there. It's possible. I think he buried the chute. I think he probably buried the briefcase. He got rid of that. I think he probably put the money in his coat and I think he headed for a big city someplace and lost himself."

If Cooper did indeed survive the jump, his first order of business would have been to survive the night. By the time he landed, it was about 8:30 in the evening and a huge storm was raging. He would have unhooked his parachutes and probably tried to hide them, which could have been quite a chore. With nothing to dig with but his hands, his best bet would have been to cover them with underbrush, or sink them if he was near a body of water. Once that was done, he would have needed to find someplace to shelter for the night, which wouldn't have been very easy either. The trees in the Northwest tend to grow tall and straight, with branches high above, so they would not have provided any sort of real shelter. In fact, they would have been lightning magnets and particularly dangerous to be near during a storm.

If Cooper lived, he would have had to hike at the beginning, and he had to figure a manhunt would quickly be underway, although in actuality, no search began until the following morning due to the weather conditions. There would've been several issues hampering Cooper's ability to hike, including perhaps his shoes. Cooper had worn business-style loafers that day, and parachutists typically prefer tightly-laced boots or athletic shoes to jump in because the speed of the fall will often rip regular shoes from their feet. As a result, Cooper may or may not have had any shoes on to walk out in. The other problem was direction; since he did not wear a watch, it seems unlikely that he thought to bring a compass. Even if he did, he had no way of knowing exactly where he was when he jumped, so he couldn't have known the best direction to go.

Some believe it's possible that Cooper did in fact start hiking through the Northwest wilderness wearing a business suit and loafers and carrying $200,000 in cash. Of course, his walk may have been hampered by an injury, because even skilled and experienced jumpers often suffer ankle injuries at some point in their careers. Cooper's chute had no mechanism to slow it down as it reached the ground, so he likely landed hard and could have even broken a bone. This would have made getting out of the forest more difficult, but not impossible.

Chapter 6: NORJAK

"The FBI learned of the crime in flight and immediately opened an extensive investigation that lasted many years. Calling it NORJAK, for Northwest hijacking, we interviewed hundreds of people, tracked leads across the nation, and scoured the aircraft for evidence. By the five-year anniversary of the hijacking, we'd considered more than 800 suspects and eliminated all but two dozen from consideration." – The FBI's website, http://www.fbi.gov/news/stories/2006/november/dbcooper_112406

"I have to confess, if I [was] going to look for Cooper, I would head for the Washougal." - FBI Chief Investigator Ralph Himmelsbach

The investigation into who D. B. Cooper was and what he was doing began as soon as Captain Scott radioed the tower and told them he was being hijacked. As a result, by the time Cooper jumped, the FBI was well-versed in the case and the investigation was underway. As soon as the passengers were freed, the FBI gathered them together and called the roll from the passenger manifest. One by one, hands went up until the agent got to the last name on the list. When he called out the name Dan Cooper, there was no response. He repeated himself twice, but no one raised a hand. Dan Cooper was the hijacker.

Next, the chief FBI agent in Portland began receiving calls from the press, asking for the name of the suspect. Clyde Jabin, a reporter with United Press International, thought he heard the answer "D. B. Cooper". Not understanding what was said through the line's static, Jabin asked, "D as in dog, B as in boy?" Distracted by weightier matters, the agent quickly said "Right" and hung up. Jabin then became the one to release the name of D. B. Cooper to the world.

At the time, the 35 passengers whom Cooper released were more confused than traumatized, and most had no idea what was actually going on until they were surrounded by agents wanting to take their statements. The big question was what Cooper looked like, because the accounts of Schaffner and those who had been near him disagreed on this point. He was definitely Caucasian and male, but beyond that, the accounts were varied and confused, as eyewitness accounts often are. Initial statements asserted that Cooper was between 30 and 50 years old, 5'8 to 6' tall, had brown eyes (Schaffner was the only one who saw him without his dark glasses on), dark black hair, and was wearing a brown or black suit.

The investigation took its next big leap when Flight 305 landed in Reno, Nevada. It was only after he safely landed the plane that Captain Scott learned his last passenger had indeed jumped. As soon as he radioed the tower with the all clear, he and his crew were swamped by FBI agents who would end up finding nothing but two of the parachutes, Cooper's tie, and some of his cigarette butts.

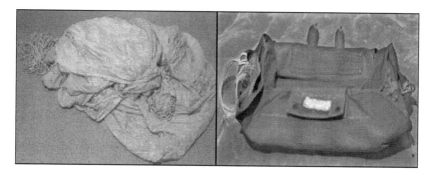

One of the parachutes left on the plane and the canvas bag it came in.

While several agents herded the flight crew away for questioning, many others boarded the plane, weighed down with cameras and evidence collection kits. The photographers went first, photographing every inch of the plane and being sure to get close-ups of where Cooper had been sitting, as well as the aft staircase and stewardess lounge. They were the first ones to discover the biggest clue Cooper forgot to take with him: his black clip-on tie with its distinctive tie clip. After snapping several photos to record where it was found, the agent stepped back and allowed a colleague to pick up the tie. After giving it a cursory examination, he placed it in an evidence bag and marked it with his initials and when and where it was found. The tie would later prove to be a key component to the investigation, because even though DNA testing was still years in the future, the agents were able to gather enough skin cells off the tie clip to eventually develop a DNA sample. While this evidence still hasn't conclusively identified a suspect, it has ruled out a number of those claiming to be or accused of being D. B. Cooper.

As the photographer moved through the cabin, the agent with the fingerprint kit followed closely, dusting armrests, magazines and door knobs for prints. Cooper had not worn gloves on the plane and had shown no concerns about leaving prints behind, which might suggest he had never been in trouble with the law before or served in the military, where his fingerprints would have been on file somewhere. Like the DNA harvested from the tie clip, the fingerprints have ruled out suspects without positively identifying one.

Along with the fingerprint technician came other agents who were searching for evidence. Every napkin, bag and glass was bagged and tagged, with special attention being paid to those items closest to where Cooper had been sitting. In addition to the two glasses he drank his bourbons from, they also found eight Raleigh cigarette butts he had left behind. His beverage choice and cigarette brand would prove to be important pieces of evidence in narrowing down the suspect list.

While some agents were questioning witnesses and others were gathering evidence, a third group of G-Men were planning the search that would begin at dawn the next morning. They questioned Scott and his crew extensively to determine as close as possible the exact time when they felt the shift in the rear of the plane. The consensus, later confirmed by a recreation of the event, was that the rear shimmy that they felt came when Cooper activated the stairway and jumped. Using maps, rulers and lots of pencil lead, they determined what they considered to be his most likely landing area, and that was where they would begin their search as soon as the sun came up.

One subject of conversation that evening was what exactly they were looking for: a fugitive or a body. The consensus among most of the trained jumpers they called in was that they would most likely find a body. The military plane that had been following closely behind Flight 305 when it left Seattle-Tacoma never saw Cooper jump and never noticed any chute opened. While they could have missed it in the dark and nearly moonless night, this added credence to the idea that Cooper's parachute never opened. Others chimed in that even if it had deployed, the forest he was jumping into was so thick that he was more likely to end up caught in a tree than landing on clear ground. Either way, the one thing everyone felt certain of that night was that they would find Cooper dead or alive. Of course, as it turned out, the investigation they had named NORJAK (the FBI's abbreviation for "Northwest Hijacking") was just beginning.

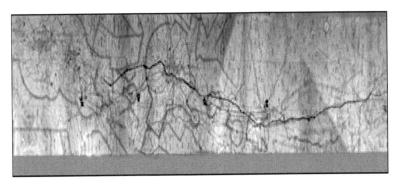

A map used by authorities trying to pinpoint where Cooper may have landed.

Beginning at dawn on November 25, Agent Ralph Himmelsbach, a licensed pilot, flew back and forth for most of the day over the area where the Bureau believed Cooper bailed out. Nonetheless, he spotted no chute in the trees, no body floating in a lake or river, no campfire smoke, and no human moving around. By the end of the day, he was worn out and happy to land, but he still figured anything he failed to find from the air would still be found quickly by the ground crew.

However, the agents working on the ground also had their work cut out for them. Divided into six teams, each covering about six square miles of terrain, they walked through the brush, and these men, most of whom were wearing heavy coats and boots, must have wondered how any man clad in Cooper's attire could make it through such thick underbrush. Their legs soon grew weary from fighting against the pull of weed and brambles, and their eyes grew tired of staring at the ground in the dim light, because even though it was the middle of the day, the thick trees above blocked out most of the sunlight.

The agents were eventually joined by law enforcement officers from around the area who were well accustomed with making searches in this terrain and had words of wisdom to offer. But even these men became discouraged when the snow began to fall. "You've got to look straight down," said one. "It sure limits the possibility of seeing anything." A sheriff speculated, "If he was smart enough to plan it out this far, he sure as hell won't leave the parachute around for us to find." An FBI agent responded grimly, "We're either looking for a parachute or a hole in the ground."

Before long, the law enforcement agents were not the only ones poking through the woods. With Cooper missing and his fate unknown, a number of people began pouring in from the surrounding area, out of curiosity or even greed. The American economy was in terrible shape at the time, and many people dreamed of finding the money and making a quick getaway with it. According to one elderly farmer, "Even a good Christian man (would keep the money). A lot of people in Clark Country are having to go on welfare because they lost their jobs. A man could buy himself a pretty nice farm with the kind of money—even if he had to go to Australia." There were also those hoping to cash in honestly by winning the $25,000 reward the airline was offering for information leading to Cooper's conviction.

Within days, the investigation entered its next inevitable phase: the crank letters. It seems that Cooper, or more likely someone pretending to be him, enjoyed taunting his pursuers. One letter chided, "I must ask you, who in the hell do some of you people think you are, and what in the hell do you think you are doing. I have succeeded in pulling off one of the most successful, talked about crimes of today…No one was endangered, the caper was only committed to show the unbelieving world that a perfect crime was possible. No harm done." Another letter painted a more tragic than glamorous picture, saying, "I didn't rob Northwest Orient because I thought it would be romantic, heroic or any of the other euphemisms that seem to attach themselves to situations of high risks. I am no modern-day Robin Hood. Unfortunately (I) do have only 14 months to live. My life has been one of hate, turmoil, hunger and more hate. This seemed to be the fastest and most profitable way to gain a few grains of peace of mind."

In the same vein, authorities quickly had to deal with copycat hijacking attempts, and when those hijackers were apprehended, they were often investigated for a possible connection to the Cooper case. McCoy's hijacking a few months later was similar enough to Cooper's that he was eyed as a possible D.B. Cooper, and books have subsequently been written arguing that Cooper was "the real McCoy".

One of the men the FBI questioned was an expert skydiver, the man who packed the four chutes offered to Cooper. They learned some interesting details from him. Most importantly, of the four chutes offered, Cooper made a very poor choice. The main chute would have been difficult to maneuver, while the secondary chute was not even a real chute; he confessed that he had accidentally given the airline agent picking up the parachutes a dummy chute by mistake. It was used in jump training but could not be deployed, so Cooper only had one working chute on him when he jumped.

The next thing the agents wanted to know was whether Cooper could have survived the fall. The skydiver assured them that Cooper could have survived but almost certainly not uninjured. By using the type of chute he chose, he almost certainly would have sustained some sort of serious injury to one or both of his legs (as one parachutist later put it, "I think he's gotta be either dead or the luckiest human in history.") With this new piece of the puzzle in hand, the FBI alerted all area hospitals to be on the lookout for any man with a broken ankle or leg.

Chapter 7: The Mystery Endures

An FBI portrait showing the suspect's possible age progression over the decades.

"When he boarded a plane in Portland, Oregon last night he was just another passenger who gave his name as D. B. Cooper. But today, after hijacking a Northwest airlines jet, ransoming the passengers in Seattle, then making a getaway by parachute somewhere between there and Reno, Nevada, the description by one wire service: Master Criminal." - Walter Cronkite

"The FBI says it has checked out nearly 1,200 potential suspects and compiled enough paperwork and reports on the case to fill a 727." – David Krajicek

By December 5, 1971, the fruitless search was winding to an end. While the FBI had their best agents and latest equipment on site, neither could hold up under the onslaught of the approaching winter. That morning, the team sent word back to their Washington headquarters: "For information of Bureau, terrain in search area varies from a ridge line which averages seventeen hundred feet and dense wood with extremely heavy undergrowth…There are many streams and hills and much of the timberland is almost impenetrable. Air search completed with negative results. A total of eight hundred square miles was covered in this search with negative results and it was noted that it consists mainly of extremely rough terrain with a number of logging roads in extremely poor condition." In other words, the area they had been searching was almost too daunting for FBI field agents and trained law enforcement officers. What chance would a man in a business suit and loafers stand of getting out alive?

With the holidays approaching and the men tired, it was time to give up this search and wait for nature to take its course. One local officer predicted, "Come next deer season some hunter will find him." On a certain level, the officer was correct, because while no one has yet found Cooper, the first piece of evidence was found by a deer hunter in 1978. It was an instruction placard on how to lower the aft stairs of a 727, and it was found lying along a little-used logging road near Castle Rock, Washington. While Cooper may have held the placard in his hand as he fell through the sky or have tucked it in his pocket as a souvenir, it seems more likely that it fell out of the airplane while the stairs were coming down and landed on the ground by itself.

The searchers returned in the spring of 1972, but they had no more luck than the initial searches months earlier. After driving his men for weeks, an army colonel finally had to give his men a break, and he ordered his aide to send a message of explanation: "Due to near exhaustion of army troops, who have endured rain, snow and other inclement weather while traversing treacherous, steep, hilly, vine, tree and brush covered areas, Lt. Col. Bonsell feels for troops' welfare and safety they should be given rest, will temporarily discontinue search." The soldiers would try to search again later, but they would again be stopped by the weather.

Over the months that followed, the physical search of the landing site would peter out as the Bureau redirected its attention toward following up on the many leads they were sent, but most of these were hoaxes, and the few legitimate possibilities never panned out. The economy continued to plummet, as did people's respect for government and law enforcement, and among the general public, those that paid any sort of attention to the case at all were likely not people who would've been inclined to rat Cooper out. The case, though still open, gradually became less and less important.

As it turned out, the FBI got its first real break nearly a decade later. In February 1980, a couple from Vancouver, Washington contacted them and turned in three bundles of money they had found along the bank of the Columbia River, about 40 miles downstream of the area the FBI had originally searched. When talking about this clue, Special Agent Carr would later admit, "The real mystery is the money. The mystery of the money is almost more interesting than the mystery of who Cooper was. If you can figure out the money, that leads you to Cooper. It's all about the money. The money is our only shot." The one thing that had plagued the agents, and still does, is that none of the money has ever turned up except for those three wet bundles.

A picture of the ransom money discovered in 1980.

Over 40 years later, the big question remains: where is D. B. Cooper today? Statistically speaking, the man who pulled off one of the most notorious hijackings in history is dead. Even if he survived the jump and lived out his life to the fullest, Cooper would now be well into his 80s. While it still strikes authorities as odd that none of the ransom money ever turned up aside from the bills discovered along the Columbia River, some have speculated that Cooper could have laundered his money at one of the many casinos that were then popping up in the 1970s on land owned by Native American tribes. Maybe D.B. Cooper died quietly, surrounded by an adoring family that never knew the truth about their relative's checkered past. That is exactly what happened to Kenny Christiansen, a man often identified as a potential suspect. Christiansen bought a house with cash just a few months after the hijacking and died in 1994, leaving behind more than $200,000 in the bank, as well as a valuable gold coin and stamp collection. Himmelsbach has discounted Christiansen as a suspect in part because he was an employee of the hijacked airline: "We had an awful lot of suggestions by people that said 'I think it's an inside job.' It is inconceivable for several reasons. The most obvious, if you know anything about airline procedure, is that it is not possible for a conspiracy to form because the individuals are not in charge of what flights they're going to go on…If you were acquainted as I was with many of the people in the airline industry, they are exceptional people. They are head and shoulders above the standards and the values and the character of normal, average Americans."

Christiansen was the only one of the many named suspects to enjoy anything close to a happily ever after kind of ending, but that's not surprising. After all, it seems unlikely that anyone who got away with such a high-profile crime would be content to sit at home and watch television for the rest of his life. Indeed, a number of the most likely suspects in the case were killed in the commission of crimes. Richard McCoy was killed in a shoot-out with the FBI after escaping from jail, and suspect John List murdered his mother, his wife and his three children just weeks before the hijacking. He remained in hiding for nearly 18 years before being caught in 1989, but while he confessed to the murders, he denied any role in the hijacking. List died in prison in 2008. Suspect Ted Mayfield also had a checkered legal history, most recently being sentenced in 2010 to three years' probation for operating an aircraft without a license. He has beaten the mortality odds so far and still lives in Sheridan, Oregon.

As David Krajicek may have best summed it up, "The crime was perfect if he lived, perfectly crazy if he didn't." Nonetheless, D.B. Cooper remains a pop culture fixture and the subject of books, movies, songs, and even commemorative events in the Pacific Northwest. Ariel, a town in Washington, celebrates Cooper Day the weekend after Thanksgiving, and other towns hold similar events, occasionally offering skydiving lessons as an appropriates reward.

While people still remain most fascinated by the case and amateurs still study the facts and evidence, Cooper's lasting legacy is felt by millions of travelers each year in airports across the country. By 1973, a device was added to the Boeing 727s that would make it impossible to activate the aft stairs while the plane was in the air, a device aptly named the Cooper Vane. More importantly, Cooper's notorious deed ultimately compelled the FAA to require the screening of passengers before they board planes. Like the hijacking case itself, most Americans are unlikely to forget about that anytime soon.

In the meantime, until the mystery of D.B. Cooper is truly solved, the search for America's most famous hijacker will continue. As one amateur sleuth put it, "I know there is something out here. There has to be."

Bibliography

Elmore, Gene. (2010) *D.B. Cooper: Aftermath.* iUniverse.

Forman, P and Forman, R. (2008) *The Legend of D.B. Cooper – Death by Natural Causes.* Borders Personal Publishing.

Grant, Walter. (2008) *D.B. Cooper, Where Are You?* Publication Consultants.

Gray, Geoffrey. (2011) *Skyjack: The Hunt for D.B. Cooper.* Crown.

Gunther, Max (1985). *D. B. Cooper: What Really Happened.* Chicago: Contemporary Books.

Himmelsbach, Ralph P.; Worcester, Thomas K. (1986). *Norjak: The Investigation of D. B. Cooper.* West Linn, Oregon: Norjak Project.

Porteous, Skipp; Blevins, Robert M. (2010). *Into the Blast – The True Story of D.B. Cooper.* Seattle, Washington: Adventure Books of Seattle.

Olson, Kay Melchisedech (2010). *D.B. Cooper Hijacking: Vanishing Act.* Compass Point Books.

Rhodes, B and Calame, R. (1991) *D.B. Cooper: The Real McCoy.* Univ. of Utah Press

Tosaw, Richard T. (1984) *D.B. Cooper: Dead or Alive?.* Tosaw Publishing.

Printed in Great Britain
by Amazon.co.uk, Ltd.,
Marston Gate.